The Inca City of Cuzco

Author: Dr. Nick Saunders

WORLD ALMANAC® LIBRARY

Please visit our web site at: www.worldalmanaclibrary.com
For a free color catalog describing World Almanac® Library's list
of high-quality books and multimedia programs, call 1-800-848-2928 (USA)
or 1-800-387-3178 (Canada). World Almanac® Library's fax: (414) 332-3567.

Library of Congress Cataloging-in-Publication Data

Saunders, Nicholas J.
   The Inca city of Cuzco / by Nick Saunders.
     p. cm. — (Places in history)
   Includes index.
   ISBN 0-8368-5812-3 (lib. bdg.)
   ISBN 0-8368-5819-0 (softcover)
   1. Cuzco (Peru : Dept.)—History—Juvenile literature.
  2. Incas—History—Juvenile literature. I. Title. II. Series.
  F3451.C9S26   2005
  985'.37—dc22   2004056927

First published in 2005 by
World Almanac® Library
330 West Olive Street, Suite 100
Milwaukee, WI 53212 USA

This U.S. edition copyright © 2005 by World Almanac® Library. Original edition copyright © 2004
ticktock Entertainment Ltd. First published in Great Britain in 2004 by ticktock Media Ltd.,
Unit 2, Orchard Business Centre, North Farm Road, Tunbridge Wells, Kent, TN2 3XF.

Consultant: Tony Morrison

Photo credits: Art Archive: 5r, 8t, 11b, 12tl, 13r, 14-15c, 16-17c, 20tr, 26-27c, 30c, 35c. Dr. Nicholas Saunders: 1, 2-3, 4b,
5bl, 6l, 7c, 10c, 11t, 12-13c, 15r, 16tl, 21t & b, 22b, 23b, 24tr, 24bl, 25all, 26cl, 27br, 29l, 31cr, 32, 33l, 33br, 34cl, 36t, 37r,
39b & cr, 40l, 45 all. Corbis: 4-5c, 6-7c, 9 all, 33tr, 34-35c, 36-37c, 38-39c, 42c, 43, 44, South American Pictures: 14t, 17br,
18-19c, 20-21tr, 20bl&r, 22tl, 23t, 24tl, 24cr, 29c, 31tl, 40b, 40-41c, 41cr, 42t.

Printed in the United States of America

1 2 3 4 5 6 7 8 9 09 08 07 06 05

Contents

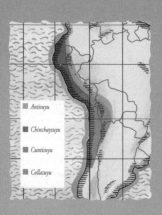

Antisuyu
Chinchaysuyu
Cuntisuyu
Collasuyu

High among the snow-capped peaks of the Andes in South America lies the ancient city of Cuzco. Designed during the 15th century, it represented not only the Inca's Earthly power and their belief in their divine right to rule but also their mythology and ancient beliefs in magical landscapes. It was from Cuzco that the Inca Empire of Tawantinsuyu—"Land of the Four Quarters"—was administered and its population of between 6 and 12 million ruled.

Creation Myths

The origins of Cuzco and the rise of the Incas are tied together. One Inca creation legend tells how originally the world was full of mountains and people who lived like wild beasts. The Sun sent two of his children, a boy and a girl, to teach them civilized ways. He instructed them to thrust a rod of solid gold into the ground wherever they stopped to eat or rest. At the spot where the rod sank easily into the Earth, they should build the sacred city of the Sun.

Eventually the boy and the girl arrived in the Valley of Cuzco, which was then just a wilderness. At the place called Huanacauri, they pushed the golden rod into the Earth, and it quickly disappeared out of sight. Convinced that this was the right place, the pair gathered together all the varied peoples of the Andean world and settled them on this spot. In this way, it was said, the great Inca city of Cuzco was filled with people.

Many ancient myths involve Lake Titicaca. In one, Viracocha the Creator gave the world light by causing the Sun and the Moon to rise from the lake.

Recorded History

Historical records tell us that, about A.D. 1438, a powerful tribe known as the Chanka attacked and defeated the Quechuas, who were allies of the Incas. The Chankas next cast an envious eye on the fertile Cuzco valley. When the Chanka attacked Cuzco, many Inca nobles panicked and fled along with their elderly chief, who was called Viracocha Inca. Two of the chief's sons, Yupanqui and Roca, stayed, along with some Inca generals, and together they fortified the town. The Chanka were eventually defeated, and the victorious Yupanqui was crowned the new Inca ruler and took the name Pachacuti. His supporters set out to conquer the many tribes of the Andes and the adjacent Pacific coast and to create what was to become ancient America's largest and most successful empire. Together with his son, Tupac Yupanqui, Yupanqui extended the empire from what today is Ecuador, in the north, to the area of the modern countries of Argentina and Chile, to the south.

Growth of an Empire

As the empire grew, the small Inca town of Cuzco was transformed. Gold, silver, precious gems, textiles, food, and manpower flowed into the city in the form of a tax called "tribute." Cuzco itself became a restricted zone, and even access to its valley was strictly controlled by the fortified gateway of Rumicolca at its southern end. With an expanding empire and many different societies to rule, Cuzco was rebuilt as a grand imperial city. Its religious buildings, such as the Coricancha (Sun Temple) and the great ceremonial plaza of Awkaypata, became the focus for grand state occasions— ceremonies and rituals designed to bind together not just Inca society but the largest and most diverse empire ever seen in ancient America.

By the 16th century, Cuzco had become fabulously wealthy. Precious metals flooded into the city, including this sumptuous silver drinking vessel.

Cuzco lies high up in the snow-capped and mist-shrouded Andes Mountains.

CHAPTER 1

How It Was Built

Cuzco was built in sacred space, in a place where land, sea, and air joined together. The city was also a physical place that had to be designed and built, incorporating the natural landscape into Inca ideas of architecture to create a powerful sense of Inca presence in the world. When Pachacuti, the first Inca emperor, handed over power to his son, Tupac Yupanqui, he turned his attention to rebuilding Cuzco as an imperial capital.

This rock shows the holes Inca builders made to put water in. When it froze, it split the stone.

matched by the magical qualities of color and luster in Inca philosophy—and all were linked to the myth of the stones that transformed into warriors at the beginning of Inca history. Cutting and shaping these raw materials demanded energy and ingenuity. Giant slabs were separated from the bedrock by drilling holes into the stone and pouring water into them. When the water froze at night, it expanded, splitting the rock into manageable chunks. These chunks were then dragged down into the valley and pulled to the building site.

Tools and Methods

Inca stonemasons had only simple tools but used careful planning and ingenuity to achieve their ends, sometimes guided by 3-D miniature models made of

Living Materials

Cuzco was built of stone. The volcanic region in which it was located offered an endless supply of different colored building materials, while limestone was also used. Many of these building blocks were hewn from quarries located in the sides of mountains that were themselves regarded as sacred and alive. For Inca stonemasons, the physical properties of building rock were

The stone ramparts at Sacsahuaman are built from polygonal blocks weighing as much as 100 tons (110.2 tonnes) each.

stone or clay. Using only different sized hammerstones, ropes, and wooden rollers, they pounded the stone into shape in or near the quarries then finished them off on-site. The exact processes used to create the impressive Inca polygonal style of wall are unknown, but the remains left at quarry sites and unfinished buildings such as those at Ollantaytambo, north of Cuzco, have left us clues. The polygonal style itself was so well conceived and built that it was

all but earthquake-proof, a quality not shared by buildings constructed of adobe (mud brick). Inca masonry blocks seem to have been lifted and levered into place using ramps and scaffolds. Stonemasons left leverage points projecting from the stones and only removed them by grinding once the stone was in the right position. Unfinished buildings sometimes have masonry blocks with leverage points still in place.

Organizing the City

Cuzco was Pachacuti's creation, conceived and built as a focus for Inca ideology and politics, as well as for the administration of the empire. Although it was a unique creation, the city's architects and builders followed ancient beliefs when designing it. It was built at

Blocks were chipped with a stone hammer to make them fit together, as shown by this illustration by Guaman Poma (1613).

the point where three rivers meet—a location long regarded by Andean peoples as a place of spiritual balance. The city was also divided into two moieties, or the symbolic halves into which traditional Andean societies were divided. The first was upper, or hanan, Cuzco. The second was lower, or hurin, Cuzco. As the city was intended as a microcosm of the four-part empire, each half contained two symbolic parts of Tawantinsuyu: hanan Cuzco included Chinchaysuyu and Antisuyu, and hurin Cuzco included Kollasuyu and Cuntisuyu. Furthermore, each of these two segments of Cuzco was home to five royal and five non-royal panaqas (clans), though in later times those living in upper Cuzco were the most powerful.

The Inca City of Cuzco

Cuzco was, therefore, an architectural expression of Inca society and the principles that organized it.

Temples and Houses

As a religious and political capital, Cuzco's finest architecture belonged to temples and shrines and the palaces and mausoleums of Inca royalty. The focus of Inca ceremonies was the Awkaypata plaza, which is dominated by an "ushnu," or throne-platform, from which the emperor presided over grand state rituals. Flanking the Awkaypata were some of Cuzco's most impressive buildings. To the southeast was the Hatunkancha, or "Great Enclosure," within which lay the Aclla Huasi, or "House of the Chosen Women." In this house were the most beautiful women in the empire, gathered together in Cuzco to serve the Inca royal family and attend to the state's religious ceremonies. A second

A 16th-century European illustration of Cuzco that shows the divisions of the city.

structure was the Amarukancha, or "Serpent Compound," which contained a great hall. On the north side of the Awkaypata was the palace-mausoleum of the emperor Huayna Capac, which, at the time of the Spanish arrival, contained the dead ruler's mummy. The locations of many other buildings of fine quality Inca masonry have been lost due to later Spanish building. Among these are a temple possibly dedicated to the god Viracocha, a large palace belonging to the emperor Huascar, another palace built by Pachacuti, and various houses belonging to members of

Tales & Customs — Lines of Power

According to legend, the power of Inca religion and mythology was imposed on the layout of Cuzco by a grid of imaginary straight lines, or ceques, *that radiated out from the Coricancha Sun Temple. They traversed the city and reached out over the summits of surrounding mountains to the empire beyond. Each line had sacred places, or* huacas, *dotted along its length—freshwater springs, tombs, and rocky outcroppings— where prayers were offered and sacrifices made to spirits and ancestors.*

the royal clans and local rulers whose lands had become part of the empire. Apart from the Coricancha (Sun Temple), there was also a temple which contained important shrines to the Illapa, the god of thunder and weather.

The Cuzco Region

The area around Cuzco was dotted with sacred places. Apart from the huge temple-fortress of Sacsahuaman, the great stone of Kenko was the center of a religious cult, and it blends natural forms with the stonemasons' skills. Situated just outside Cuzco, Kenko is a huge rocky outcropping that has been intricately carved with zig-zag channels and steps, underneath which are the remains of a rock-cut passage that may have been a tomb. This place may have been the focus of ancestor worship for the emperor Pachacuti. Adjacent to the stone is a circle of high quality Inca

Inca walls stand in the Courtyard of the Serpents in Cuzco, Peru, which is built on the site of the Palace of the Inca, Huayna Capac.

stonework that encloses a monolith. The Stone of Sayhuite is a similar carved-stone boulder that is decorated with carvings that portray a symbolic landscape—perhaps an image of the Inca universe. A scene containing human beings, maize plants, mountain lions, monkeys, and birds is carved into the rock's surface. In Inca philosophy, stone was matched by water in terms of its magical qualities

and importance. The two came together in canals and springs where water flowed along cut-stone channels. At Tambo Machay, also near Cuzco, a natural spring has been tapped and channeled by a system of intricate Inca stonework—part of the sacred flow of water around the Inca capital and in this case its surroundings.

The dramatic Kenko stone is thought to be the death house of the emperor Pachacuti.

Cuzco rapidly grew from a small village to the largest and most sophisticated city of pre-Columbian South America. When the Spanish arrived in the 16th century, they made the city of Lima, located on Peru's Pacific coast, their capital. But Cuzco retained its symbolic importance. Today, Cuzco and its surrounding area is Peru's center of tourism. It is a museum of Inca culture and a point of departure for those visiting the mountaintop Inca city of Machu Picchu.

A view of the inside of the great temple of Coricancha, sacred heart of Cuzco.

While Pachacuti Inca was the first true emperor, his predecessors were probably little more than chiefs in the Cuzco region and they remain shadowy figures. It is impossible to establish accurate dates for these first Inca rulers, though a starting point for the Inca dynasty about A.D. 1200 is usually accepted.

A Multicultural City

Cuzco was transformed as Pachacuti's armies conquered large areas of the Andes and the adjacent Pacific coast. War booty and tribute wealth flowed into the city. In 1463, Pachacuti handed control of the army to his son, Tupac Yupanqui, and

The Early Years

Little is known about the early years of Cuzco and its people. Unfortunately, the Incas did not keep written records. Our information comes mainly from the Spanish, who interviewed the Incas after the conquest of 1532 and who wrote to put themselves in a favorable light. Also, the information the Incas gave to the Spanish was contradictory, as it mixed myth and history.

Time Line

1438	Pachacuti Inca defeats the Chanca and becomes emperor.
1463	Pachacuti's son, Tupac Yupanqui, takes command of the army, and Pachacuti begins rebuilding Cuzco as a grand imperial capital.
1471	Tupac Yupanqui succeeds Pachacuti.
1493	Huayna Capac succeeds Tupac Yupanqui as emperor.
1527	Huayna Capac dies without naming an heir. His son, Huascar, is recognized as emperor in Cuzco, but a rival, Atahualpa, is championed in Quito.

turned his attention to redesigning and rebuilding Cuzco as an awe-inspiring imperial capital. As Inca military victories expanded the empire, conquered leaders and craftspeople were brought to Cuzco, making it a cosmopolitan city of several thousand people. When the Kingdom of Chimor, on Peru's north coast, fell to the Inca about 1470, its master goldsmiths were taken to Cuzco to work for the Inca on adorning the city's temples with statues and masks

The remains of an Inca road into Cuzco reflect the city's importance as a trading center.

of solid gold. Expert stone workers from the area around Lake Titicaca were brought to Cuzco and Ollantaytambo to construct some of the empire's most stunning buildings. The sons of conquered leaders were honored to live in Cuzco and learn Inca ways but, in fact, were also high status hostages. Temples dedicated to the Inca deities, palace-mausoleums for the

emperors, great open plazas for grand state occasions, and numerous smaller shrines, as well as the invisible ceque lines of power, were all integrated into the city's design. For the Incas, Cuzco was the mirror of heaven—its layout, monumental buildings, and royal inhabitants were all organized by their ideas about religion and cosmology. At its zenith, Cuzco probably had about 100,000 inhabitants. It represented a microcosm of the empire whose wealth paid for it—a miniature of the Inca cosmos in whose buildings dwelt the gods and human rulers of Tawantinsuyu.

These gold and silver figures show the skill of the Inca craftspeople brought to work in Cuzco.

The Inca City of Cuzco

This 20th-century painting shows Spanish conquistador Francisco Pizarro.

The Spanish Arrival

In 1532, Spanish conquistadors under Francisco Pizarro invaded the Inca Empire, and in the northern town of Cajamarca quickly captured Atahualpa, the victor in the recent civil war against his rival, Huascar. With Atahualpa (who was later executed) held hostage, Pizarro sent three conquistadors to Cuzco in early 1533 to oversee the stripping of the city's gold as ransom for the Inca leader.

They marveled at what they found and ripped off seven hundred great sheets of gold from the rooms of the Coricancha temple of Inti. They took possession of the city for the King of Spain and locked up a house full of treasure that they couldn't carry. On November 15, 1533, having marched south from Cajamarca, Pizarro and the main Spanish force defeated an Inca army on the hills surrounding Cuzco and entered the capital. Ever the opportunist, Pizarro claimed he had come to liberate Cuzco from Atahualpa's warriors, who had occupied it after the civil war and to return it to Huascar's family in the person of the Inca prince Manco Capac, who had recently joined Huascar. Pizarro's men soon began looting the astonishing wealth of Cuzco's temples and royal palaces—gold and silver statues, more gold temple cladding, and unusual items such as shoes and crayfish fashioned from gold and jewels. They also discovered storehouses full of food, drink, clothing, weapons, and even deposits of delicate iridescent hummingbird feathers used by the Inca upper classes as markers of their high social status. The precious metal treasures were melted down, one-fifth set aside for the Spanish Crown, and the rest divided up between the conquistadors.

Manco the Puppet

During these early days in Cuzco, the Spanish were careful to keep their puppet ruler, Manco Capac, and the city's inhabitants quiet and content. Pizarro allowed Manco to be crowned Manco Inca in festivities that lasted thirty days and involved much drinking and celebration. The sacred mummies of Manco's royal predecessors were paraded through the city, and music, song, and prayers were addressed to the god Inti. Pizarro and his men thus had a unique and first-hand view of the most impressive Inca ritual virtually untouched by Spanish influence. In the months that

Time Line		
1527–1532	Civil war between Huascar and Atahualpa.	
1532	Atahualpa wins civil war. His soldiers occupy Cuzco. The Spanish arrive.	
1533	Huascar is executed on Atahualpa's orders. Atahualpa executed by Francisco Pizarro. Tupac Huallpa becomes puppet emperor	and is assassinated. Manco Capac (later named Manco Inca) replaces Tupac Huallpa.
1534		Cuzco is founded as a Spanish and Christian city by the conquistador Francisco Pizarro.
1536–1537		Siege of Cuzco by the Incas.

12

followed, the Spanish tightened their grip on Cuzco, began rebuilding it as a colonial city, and treated Manco and his family with increasing humiliation and brutality in their efforts to extort ever more Inca treasure. This gold fever was to have tragic consequences.

The Inca Siege of Cuzco

In 1536, Manco Inca was allowed to leave Cuzco by Francisco Pizarro's brother, Hernando. The emperor had promised to bring more hidden Inca gold to the Spanish but instead escaped to the mountains and was joined by an Inca army which had been raised in secret. The Incas camped on the hills surrounding Cuzco, besieging the two hundred Spanish soldiers in the city. In May of that year, Manco's warriors attacked, bitterly fighting their way through the city's narrow streets and

Tiny gold or silver figures dressed in woven mantles were among the many treasures seized by the invading Spanish.

This 18th-century Cuzco School painting shows Atahualpa, who became undisputed Inca ruler in 1532.

setting fire to the thatched roofs with burning slingstones. In just a few days, Cuzco was a smoking ruin, and the Incas were on the verge of a stunning victory against the Spanish.

The remaining Spanish soldiers gambled everything on one reckless move. After spending a night in prayer, fifty cavalrymen broke out of the city and, aided by their Amerindian allies, recaptured the heights in front of the great temple-fortress of Sacsahuaman.

The Inca City of Cuzco

The Inca site of Ollantaytambo was one of the last strongholds of Manco Inca.

Fierce hand-to-hand fighting continued for days, with attacks, repulses, and counterattacks. Eventually the Spaniards used scaling ladders to capture the fortress and then massacred the surviving Inca warriors. This was a critical moment. While Cuzco remained under Inca siege for another ten months, and several Spanish rescue missions were wiped out, the Inca army could never again break back into the city. Finally, Manco's warriors began drifting back to the land to harvest their crops, and Francisco Pizarro's compatriot Don Diego de Almagro relieved the siege in April 1537. From this point onward, Cuzco had become a Spanish, not an Inca, city.

The End of Inca Cuzco

While Cuzco was now controlled by the Spanish, Manco Inca remained defiant in the town of Ollantaytambo, a two day march to the north. Chased by the Spaniards, the fugitive Manco Inca escaped first to Vitcos and then moved deeper into the tropical forests at Vilcabamba, a week of hard marching to the northwest of Cuzco. For six years, Manco lived with his followers at Vilcabamba, until he was murdered by five Spanish conquistadors to whom he had given sanctuary. Several of Manco's sons then ruled for short periods and were, in turn, succeeded by another son, Tupac Amaru.

In 1572, a new Spanish viceroy arrived in Peru. Francisco de Toledo was determined to destroy Vilcabamba once and for all and remove all possibility of future rebellion. In June of that year, he marched north and finally smashed his way into Vilcabamba, where he found only an abandoned city whose temples and buildings were still smoking from having been set on fire by the fleeing Incas.

Toledo's men finally caught up with Tupac Amaru while he was sitting with his wife around a campfire. The Spanish expedition returned to Cuzco in tri-

umph, dragging Tupac Amaru behind them in chains, along with a golden statue of Inti and the sacred mummies of Manco Inca and one of his sons, Titu Cusi Yupanqui. The scene was set for Cuzco to play out the last tragic act of the conquest with the execution of Tupac Amaru.

Death of an Emperor

On the appointed day, the Spaniards in Cuzco reported that the air was full of the wailing of grieving Incas who had gathered in thousands inside the city and on the surrounding hills. Even some Spanish were said to have wept openly for the last Inca emperor. The bells of Cuzco's recently built churches and monasteries began to toll, and Tupac was decapitated, ending the imperial royal dynasty that had begun with Pachacuti and Tupac Yupanqui.

Tupac Amaru, the son of Manco Yupanqui, was executed by the Spanish in 1572.

Spanish Colonial Cuzco

The Spanish had begun reshaping Inca Cuzco almost as soon as they arrived in 1533, although the basic Inca city plan was preserved throughout the colonial period. After looting the temples and palaces, they began to destroy or rebuild the obviously religious Inca structures. Other changes occurred when Inca palaces were assigned to high-ranking Spanish soldiers for their own use and adapted to a European style of living. Other areas were given to soldiers for house building, and other spaces were designated for public use. The Inca's great ceremonial plaza of Awkaypata became the plaza of the colonial city. On

Poma's illustration shows the emperor Topa Inca being led in chains to Cuzco for execution.

The Inca City of Cuzco

This photograph shows how the Spanish often built their houses directly on top of Inca buildings.

March 23, 1534, Francisco Pizarro officially founded Cuzco as a Spanish and Christian city, and in 1540, Cuzco was permitted to call itself "the head of the kingdoms of Peru." This preeminence was based on its antiquity and prestige as capital of the Inca empire. The building of churches and monasteries achieved several ends. Not only did it aid the conversion of the Incas and other indigenous peoples to Christianity, but it also removed any possible focus for rebellion based on the Inca's sacred buildings. Spanish recon-

struction was also facilitated by the great fire that raged through the city during Manco Inca's siege in 1536 and again by a serious earthquake in 1650, after which further rebuilding was undertaken.

Replacing the Old

Taking advantage of the superb architecture created by Inca stonemasons, the Spanish built many of their buildings by re-using Inca masonry or simply constructing a colonial building on an Inca base. Today, visitors still marvel at buildings which seem to straddle two worlds. The most famous example is the Coricancha temple to Inti, the upper parts of which were dismantled and the interior remodeled to become the Dominican monastery of Santo Domingo. The great temple-fortress of Sacsahuaman became a quarry site during the 16th and 17th centuries, its beautifully carved stones removed by Inca laborers in order to build private houses for the Spanish in Cuzco. The

This 18th-century painting depicts Tupac Amaru being taken prisoner by Spaniards.

ruins of Sacsahuaman represented the ruination of the Inca cult of Inti and the triumph of Jesus Christ. Perhaps the ultimate symbol of the Christianization of Cuzco was the building of the city's first church on the spot where the Virgin Mary was said to have appeared during Manco Inca's siege of the city. Using stones from Sacsahuaman, Cuzco's cathedral was built next to this church and was opened in 1654. Apart from recycling the great stone-built Inca buildings,

Time Line

1932	Archaeological excavations at Sacsahuaman and the surrounding area mark the 400th anniversary of the Spanish conquest.	
1933	Cuzco is designated the "archaeological capital of South America."	

1946	Modern Inti Raymi festival devised by Cuzco journalist Humberto Vidal Unda. Today the festival attracts thousands of tourists each year.	
1950	Major earthquake strikes city, revealing sturdy Inca remains beneath more fragile Spanish buildings.	

Tupac Amaru II's supporters fought not only the royalist forces but also other indigenous groups who had sided with the royalists. When the rebel leader failed to surround Cuzco, the initiative was lost, and Cuzco's defenders gained the upper hand. Tupac Amaru II was captured in April 1781 and executed soon after.

colonial Cuzco was also rebuilt using cheaper Sun-baked bricks (adobes) in a way that was nowhere near as resistant to the region's earthquakes.

The Rebellion of Tupac Amaru II

Despite the attempts of the Spanish to avoid rebellions of the native peoples of the Andes by controlling their everyday lives and converting them to Christianity, violent uprisings did occur. The most serious was in 1780, when a curaca from near Cuzco took the name Tupac Amaru II, after the last Inca emperor, killed a local official, and attracted local peasants to his cause by proclaiming the return of the Inca. Tupac Amaru II's men defeated royal soldiers sent to crush them and marched on Cuzco itself. The city was besieged in early 1781, and thousands died in the conflict.

1970	UNESCO (United Nations Educational, Scientific, and Cultural Organization) sponsored investigations of the city begin.
1983	UNESCO declares Cuzco a World Heritage site. The Peruvian government declares Cuzco is the tourist capital of Peru.
1993	The Peruvian government designates Cuzco as the historical capital of Peru. Excavation of the Sacred Garden is completed.

The Dominican monastery of Santo Domingo was built directly over Coricancha.

17

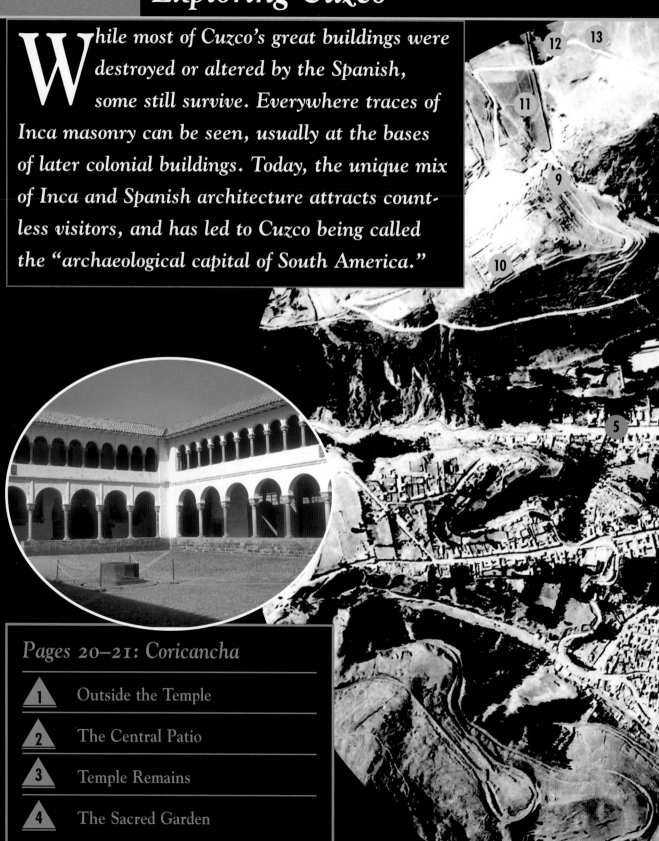

While most of Cuzco's great buildings were destroyed or altered by the Spanish, some still survive. Everywhere traces of Inca masonry can be seen, usually at the bases of later colonial buildings. Today, the unique mix of Inca and Spanish architecture attracts countless visitors, and has led to Cuzco being called the "archaeological capital of South America."

12

13

11

9

10

5

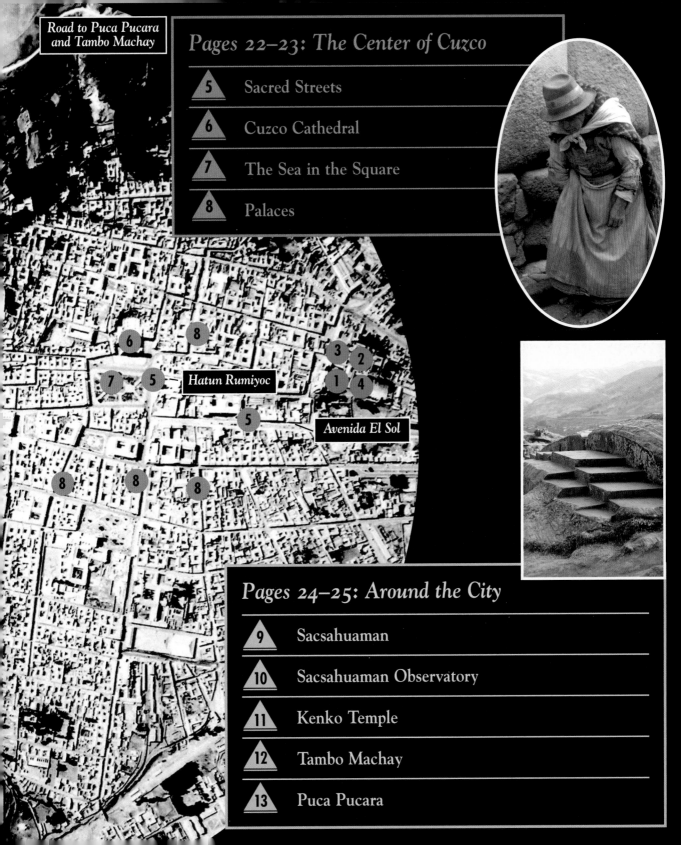

Road to Puca Pucara
and Tambo Machay

Hatun Rumiyoc

Avenida El Sol

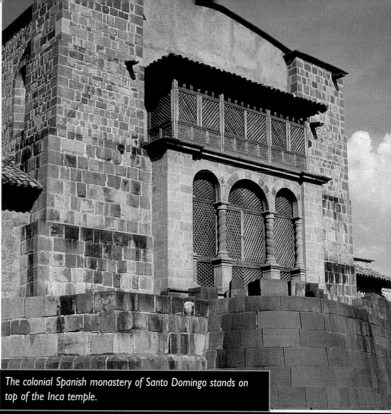

1 Outside the Temple

Today, as in Inca times, central Cuzco is dominated by the Coricancha, the golden house of the Sun-god, Inti. As you approach the building, it appears to be a striking mix of styles—the Spanish colonial church of Santo Domingo built on a curving semicircular base of high-quality Inca masonry blocks.

The colonial Spanish monastery of Santo Domingo stands on top of the Inca temple.

2 The Central Patio

Passing through the colonial entrance, you enter the central patio. Around the sides of the patio are paintings produced by the anonymous artists of the School of Cuzco and the remains of the original Inca building, which had been dismantled and covered up when the original church and monastery of Santo Domingo was built. Only after the destruction of parts of the Spanish church during the 1950 earthquake were many of the remaining Inca structures rediscovered. Originally, Coricancha featured five fountains that channeled sacred water around the buildings.

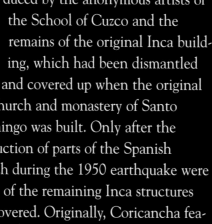

This view of the central patio shows a fountain that was unearthed by archaeologists.

One of the School of Cuzco paintings that surround the central patio.

Temple Remains

In the Coricancha complex, there were temples to different Inca deities, such as the Moon-goddess Mama Quilla, whose walls were covered in silver and around whose central image were positioned the sacred mummies of past Inca queens. The main building, however, was dedicated to Inti, with a huge image of the Sun-god in the

Part of the remains of the Inca temples of Coricancha.

form of a great face surrounded by Sun rays. Arrayed on either side of the Inti image were the mummies of past Inca kings, each set on a golden litter. Unfortunately, only a few walls of these temples remain today.

Part of the Sacred Garden that lies outside the walls of Coricancha.

The Sacred Garden

Outside, in front of the curving Inca temple walls, are the remains of the "sacred garden," a miniature landscape in which every kind of life known to the Incas—including llamas, birds, and snakes—was modeled in gold, silver, and jewels. A full-time silversmith was dedicated to making these items. All of these treasures were quickly looted and melted down by the Spanish. The garden area itself, however, was covered up with miscellaneous buildings until it was cleared and excavated during the 1980s.

The Inca City of Cuzco

An elderly Quechua walks down Cuzco's Hatun Rumiyoc.

 ## Sacred Streets

Hatun Rumiyoc is one of the best preserved and most impressive of Inca Cuzco's streets. Its finely carved polygonal masonry is typical of the skill lavished by Inca stonemasons on the capital's most important constructions. Apart from the quality of its stonework, there is no other indication that Hatun Rumiyoc street marks the important dividing line between the two sacred halves of the city—hanan, or upper, Cuzco and hurin, or lower, Cuzco.

 ## Cuzco Cathedral

On the north side of the Plaza Mayor is Cuzco's colonial cathedral. In Inca times, it was probably the location of the palace of the creator-deity Viracocha and, thus, an obvious target for Spanish destruction and rebuilding as a Christian place of worship. In the space adjacent to it is the spot where the Virgin Mary was said to have appeared to the Spanish during Manco Inca's siege of the city in 1536. It was in this place that Cuzco's first church was built. This church was later incorporated into the larger cathedral, the construction of which began in 1559 and was completed nearly a century later, in 1654. To build the cathedral, huge stones were brought from the quarry of Rumicolca, south of the city. Stones were also brought from Sacsahuaman, moved from an Inca religious site to a Christian site.

The impressive front of Cuzco's colonial cathedral.

A modern view of the Plaza Mayor, once the site for many Cuzco rituals.

The Sea in the Square

Today, the Plaza Mayor of the Spanish colonial city is on the spot once occupied by the great Inca square called Awkaypata, which was the location of many of the grand state rituals of Inca times. Originally, the floor of the plaza was covered with a deep layer of sand brought up from the Pacific coast, which symbolized the far-reaching power of the Inca. It also expressed a mythic link with the idea of the sea as the "Mother of Fertility" in Inca philosophy. The sand was removed by the Spanish in 1559 when it was found that local people considered it sacred and hid valuable offerings in it. The sand was reused in building the cathedral and local bridges.

Palaces

When Francisco Pizarro arrived in Cuzco in 1533, he immediately gave the best Inca buildings to his men, who began altering them for a European lifestyle. During the following years, many Spanish-style houses were built with recycled Inca masonry or with adobe mud bricks resting on an Inca base. Often they also had Spanish-style wooden balconies.

For this house, like many houses in modern Cuzco, Spanish architecture literally lies on top of Incan styles.

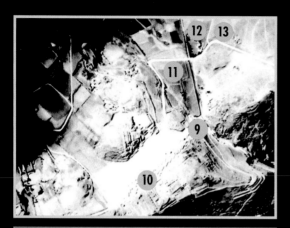

Part of the surviving ramparts of Sacsahuaman, overlooking Cuzco city.

 ## Sacsahuaman

Inca-Spanish Sacsahuaman stands on a rocky outcropping on Cuzco's outskirts. Much of the best-quality stonework at this site was removed by the Spanish to provide building stone for colonial-period Cuzco. The fifth ceque (sacred line) of the Chinchaysuyu quarter of the empire radiated out of Coricancha and passed over Sacsahuaman to the nearby rock known as Suchuna. Suchuna was carved by the Incas into a series of low, flat steps. It is popularly known as the "Inca Throne" because its steps appear to be low-lying seats. This shrine was venerated and sacrificed to in its own right and was thought to be so sacred that the whole fortress of Sacsahuaman was also worshiped because of its proximity to Suchuna.

The "Inca Throne" was exquisitely carved out of stone and worshiped by Incans.

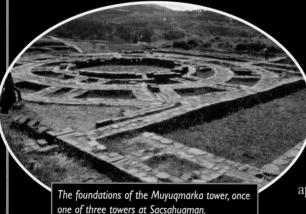

The foundations of the Muyuqmarka tower, once one of three towers at Sacsahuaman.

Sacsahuaman Observatory

All that is left of the great Muyuqmarka tower—which once dominated Sacsahuaman's skyline—are its impressive circular foundations. There were once three towers, but Pucamarca and Sallaqmarca have long since disappeared, their stones taken by Spanish builders.

11 Kenko Temple

The Kenko Temple is on a small hill called Socorro, at the edge of Sacsahuaman. The site has two parts. One is the great carved rock, and the other is a semicircular plaza. In the rock section, there is a natural formation on which figures— including animals, such as reptiles and felines, and two cylindrical figures or shapes—are carved. Less than 1,640 feet (500 meters) away is Little Kenko, a small site with a series of carved rocks and stone seats. The monument is surrounded by a wall with granite stones laid in a cell-shaped manner.

Kenko stone, located just outside Cuzco.

12 Tambo Machay

This picture shows one of the water springs that flows into the famous Inca's Bath.

Located about 5.6 miles (9 kilometers) from Cuzco, the main feature of this site is two water springs that flow through carved stones into a pool known as the Inca's Bath. This site was probably once a temple dedicated to the worship of water. It was also probably the starting point of a network of waterways used to irrigate the peasants' terraces. In the past, Tambo Machay was also a hunting lodge for the Inca Yupanqui and may have been a site for human sacrifice. The site can be reached by foot or by horse from Sacsayhuaman.

13 Puca Pucara

About 4.3 miles (7 km) from the city of Cuzco is the archaeological complex of Puca Pucara. Puca Pucara was once a housing complex and food storeroom. The stone building on the site has interior plazas, bathrooms, aqueducts, and an old road that is easily recognizable.

The stone walls of the Puca Pucara complex.

During Inca times, Cuzco was a city where imperial religion and the administration of the empire came together. The royal clans (panaqas), priests, administrators, and bureaucrats rubbed shoulders with specialist craftspeople and the families of local rulers who had been conquered by the Incas and absorbed into the empire.

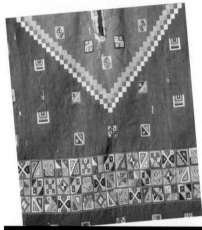

A blue Inca poncho with geometrical designs that was worn by high-status people in Cuzco.

The Inca Emperor and His Queen

The Inca emperor claimed descent from the Sun god Inti through the founding ancestor Manco Capac. Known as the Sapa Inca (Unique Inca), the emperor was Inti's divine representative on Earth, and all his subjects were symbolically regarded as either his sons or his wives. The succession of an Inca emperor was a pragmatic affair. Officially, the eldest legitimate son became emperor, but in fact, the most able was usually chosen.

In order to keep royal blood as pure as possible, the emperor alone was permitted to marry his own full sister. It was only from the children of this marriage that a new emperor could be chosen. Apart from his sister-wife, the Sapa Inca possessed hundreds of concubines and secondary wives with whom he had numerous children. None of these, however, were allowed to become emperor. Being an Inca emperor was a highly individual undertaking. Every new emperor built his own royal palace in Cuzco and had it furnished with his own possessions. When he died, his palace became a mausoleum housing his royal mummy, supported by revenues from his estates, and looked after by his family and clan.

A Godly Figure

As the emperor was regarded as a divine being, access to his royal person was strictly controlled. Even the highest official had to remove his sandals, place a symbolic burden on his back, and

26

Tales & Customs — Dawn over Lake Titicaca

Among the Incas, Lake Titicaca was widely regarded as the origin of human beings. They believed that, out of the primordial darkness, the creator-god, Viracocha, created light, causing the Sun to rise from the lake and the Moon and stars to ascend into the heavens. The god cried out to the Inca leader Manco Capac, foretelling how his people would be great warriors and conquer the world he had brought into being.

approach his monarch with lowered eyes. Sometimes the emperor was physically separated from his audience, seated on a stool behind a screen. For those allowed to gaze

An 18th-century Cuzco School painting showing Manco Capac shown holding the Sun.

upon the divine body, the emperor was recognizable by the way he was dressed. He wore the finest quality clothing and a multicolored braiding, known as the llauta, as a headband. Tassles of vicuña wool dyed red and decorated with gold hung from the llauta onto the emperor's forehead as a fringe called the borla.

The Royal Court

The emperor's royal court was characterized by ritual and hierarchy. In Cuzco, his every need was attended to by his concubine wives, who fed him from gold and silver plates. Traveling around the city and the empire, he was carried on a magnificent litter decorated with gold and jewels and supported by twenty men. The emperor himself sat behind a curtain, invisible to his subjects. Keeping out of sight allowed him to maintain an aura of mystery and power.

The Sapa Inca's official wife was known as the Coya (Queen), and she was also his sister. As the sacred wife of a sacred god-emperor, the Coya had religious duties that complemented those of her husband. She was the high priestess of the Inca cult of the Moon, and she was responsible for prayers, festivals, and the maintenance of the female deity's shrines.

An illustration by Guaman Poma showing the emperor and family being carried around by his servants.

This 18th-century painting shows the wedding of Inca princess Nusta Beatriz to a Spanish noble.

The association of the Moon's phases and the passing seasons meant that the Coya was especially concerned with matters of agriculture, animal husbandry, and fertility more widely. In Cuzco, the Coya's royal garden was a symbolic landscape full of the empire's varied species of plants and animals. As the Coya's role was both ideological and religious, she kept a palace in Cuzco in which her royal banner—a multi-colored rainbow—was displayed.

As with her husband, the Coya was considered a figure of purity. As such she bathed several times a day, wore articles of clothing no more than once, and ate alone. Walking around the city, her servants placed new cumbi cloth in her path so that she never trod the Earth of lesser mortals. She was attended by her own female servants of royal blood, called *ñusta*, who catered for her every wish.

Tales & Customs — Growing Up Inca

The rites of Huarachico were part of December's Capac Raymi festivities, during which noble Inca boys underwent the passage into manhood. These puberty rites took place when boys were fourteen years old and included making numerous sacrifices to the gods at different locations around the city. They took part in a 1,000-meter race and were finally given the signs of adulthood—a breechcloth and gold earlobe-plugs. Simpler celebrations took place for the boys of lower social classes.

Inca Royalty

Beneath the Sapa Inca and his Coya were the members of the royal clans, who were connected to the emperor by ties of blood and kinship. It was from this group that the empire's four royal prefects were recruited, each controlling one of the four quarters (suyus) into which the empire was divided. These individuals also formed the Inca's Supreme Council of advisors. These hereditary nobles shared their high status with another group known as "Incas-by-privilege." This second group was composed of local non-Inca people who nevertheless shared the Inca's Quechua language and had been related to the Inca emperors before the rule of Pachacuti Inca by political marriages and alliances. Their privileged status was a reward for having supported the Incas before their rise to power. They were also needed to fill offices of state as the empire and the demand for trusted manpower grew. Both groups displayed their high social position by their appearances, especially

This illustration by Guaman Poma shows granaries supervised by a curaca.

the large earlobe-plugs that led the Spanish to refer to them as "Orejones" or "Big Ears." Some Incas-by-privilege were settled in distant parts of the empire, teaching Inca culture by example and instructing newly conquered peoples in the Inca way of doing things. Other members of this group stayed in Cuzco and were organized into ten ayllus, or kin groups.

The Curaca

The curaca were the indigenous lords of areas that had been conquered by the Incas. After a military victory, imperial Inca policy permitted local leaders to retain power and rule in the Sapa Inca's name. The curaca were a kind of secondary nobility, but unlike the hereditary nobles and Incas-by-privilege, they were never allowed to call themselves Incas or wear exactly the same clothing or jewelry. The curacas mainly administered the empire as a grassroots part of the imperial bureaucracy that was in charge of collecting taxes from groups of one hundred or more people.

This figure shows the stretched earlobes caused by the metal earlobe-plugs worn by Inca men of a high status. The eyes and the midriff of the figure are made from a sacred pink seashell called spondylus, while the figure also contains gold and amethyst bands.

The Inca City of Cuzco

The Priesthood

Serving the Inca gods was an elaborate priesthood about which very little is known because they were targets for Spanish accusations of devil worship and paganism. In general, the priesthood seems to have reflected Inca society, with the top level being drawn from the royal family of the emperor. In Cuzco, at the time of the Spanish arrival, the office of the high priest of Inti was called Villac Umu, an official whose title meant "slave of the Sun." Almost as powerful in religious matters as the emperor, the position of Villac Umu was held for life. Beneath him, the Inca empire was divided into ten religious areas, or dioceses, each of which was presided over by a chief priest called Hatun Villca. These individuals were in charge of all other priests who were lower down the scale and were responsible for making sacrifices, interpreting oracles, praying, curing illness, and managing the cult of the dead. Lower still were diviners who predicted the future with maize grains or spiders that they kept in hollow human bones and then observed how they fell to the ground. Women also served as priestesses, especially to the cults of the Sun and Moon. As these duties required purity of body and spirit, they were not allowed to marry.

This detail from an 18th-century Cuzco-school painting of a Corpus Christi festival depicts an Inca prince (shown wearing a headdress) with a priest.

The Sacred Women

One of the most extraordinary inventions of the Inca empire was the institution of the sacred women who were regarded as part of the priesthood. They were called acllas, or chosen women, and are sometimes referred to as the "Virgins of the Sun." Their everyday life and behavior was supervised by elder women, the mama cunas, or mothers. The aclla were young Inca maidens who served the cult of Inti the Sun-god in Cuzco. They tended the royal mummies of past emperors and queens as well as looked after the daily needs of the current royal family. Brought to the capital from all over the empire, they were selected for their physical beauty and perfection at the age of ten and lived cloistered in convents called aclla huasi. Some prepared the clothing, food, and chicha beer for the Inca, while others had similar responsibilities for the grand state occasions during which the gods and rulers were worshiped. Their duties varied according to their roles, but included spinning, dyeing, and weaving the fine cloth known as cumbi used by royalty and offered to the gods. Some aclla took a vow of chastity in honor

The restored adobe ruins of the Virgins of the Sun complex at Pachacamac. Similar complexes of the Virgins of the Sun once stood at Cuzco.

of Inti and were given the important symbolic duty of guarding the sacred fire for the Inti Raymi festival. The high priestess of the aclla was a high-ranking noblewoman who was regarded as the symbolic wife of Inti. Some acllas were chosen to be concubines for the emperor. These women were also used on occasion as a tool of imperial policy, given by the emperor to foreign dignitaries with whom the Inca wished to form political marriage alliances.

Keepers of the Quipu

The Inca Empire was a multi-ethnic creation with a population of between six and twelve million people. The various groups of the empire included those who lived in high mountain valleys, arid coastal deserts, and tropical rain forests. To administer this numerous and multilingual population, the Inca developed a large and efficient bureaucracy of which the most famous were the quipu camayoc—the keepers of the quipu.

Quipu were knotted strings used for keeping records of births, marriages, deaths, taxation, dates, laws, punishments, the decisions of oracles, and details of the economic production of particular areas. Quipu fulfilled the record-keeping functions of alphabetic writing, which the Inca did not possess. They seem to have functioned as mnemonic aids, depending on knowledge of a quipu camayoc for their interpretation.

Quipus were widely used throughout Peru for counting purposes. Many survive today, and historians are learning more about the way they worked (see pages 40-41).

Tales & Customs — Magical Stones

According to Inca legend, the Chanka attack on Cuzco was finally repulsed when stones and rocks known as pururaucas rose up and magically turned into warriors to fight with the Incas against their enemies. After the victory, they changed back into their original shapes. In gratitude for their supernatural help, the emperor Pachacuti gathered them up and placed them in the city's shrines, where they were worshiped.

The Inca City of Cuzco

Inca commoners were responsible for tending the land. They grew crops on terraces like the ones shown above.

The Commoners

At the bottom of Inca society was the mass of ordinary people. These commoners were mainly engaged in agriculture, and they paid their taxes with a mixture of goods and services to the state and their local communities. The main burden of the commoners were the different kinds of labor tax, or mita, that they were expected to pay. They cultivated the lands of the emperor and those belonging to the official state religion of Inti, in addition to cultivating their own small holdings. The commoners also had to spend time maintaining the infrastructure of the empire by building bridges, constructing roads, and serving in the army. Some were more fortunate than others and paid their taxes by working as specialists in metalworking, woodworking, or pottery-making for the upper classes.

The position of quipu camayoc was hereditary, passing from father to son, but was also regarded as a profession by the Inca. Being a quipu camayoc demanded constant practice, and the detailed knowledge required was taught to the younger officials by the older, more experienced ones. This knowledge included how to make a quipu, where to place a knot on one of its colored strings, how to use the combination of knots, colors, and strings to record information, and how to remember it by memorizing its details. Whether or not the quipu system was really an alternative to writing is debated by experts. Some experts interpret the evidence as indicating that each quipu camayoc could read and remember only the quipu that he had made and that, therefore, using quipus was not a true alternative to writing.

Tales & Customs — Population Survival

The Spanish conquest had a devastating effect on the Inca population of Peru. By the end of the 16th century, the Inca population had fallen from between 8 and 10 million because of fighting and disease. Many Incas were forced by their Spanish rulers to work in mines and on plantations. Today, however, there are still 3 million Quechua, descendants of the Inca, who carry on the traditions of their ancestors.

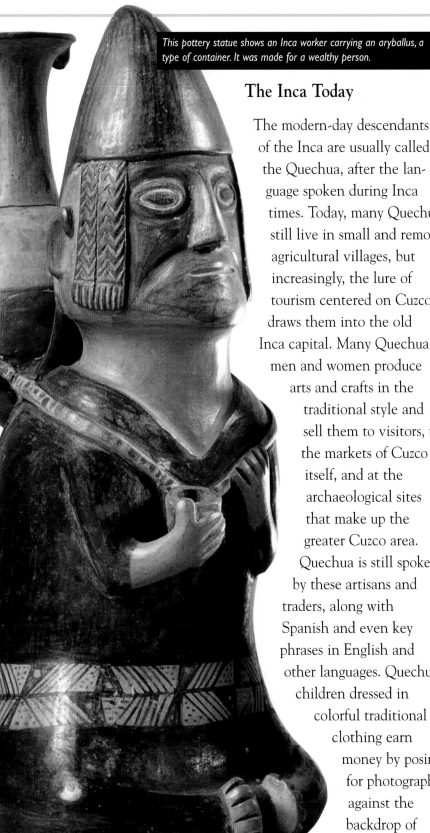

This pottery statue shows an Inca worker carrying an aryballus, a type of container. It was made for a wealthy person.

The Inca Today

The modern-day descendants of the Inca are usually called the Quechua, after the language spoken during Inca times. Today, many Quechua still live in small and remote agricultural villages, but increasingly, the lure of tourism centered on Cuzco draws them into the old Inca capital. Many Quechua men and women produce arts and crafts in the traditional style and sell them to visitors, to the markets of Cuzco itself, and at the archaeological sites that make up the greater Cuzco area. Quechua is still spoken by these artisans and traders, along with Spanish and even key phrases in English and other languages. Quechua children dressed in colorful traditional clothing earn money by posing for photographs against the backdrop of Inca buildings.

Quechua women preserve the art of weaving and sell their products to visitors to Cuzco.

A Quechua girl sits in Incan ruins posing for tourists.

Life in Inca Cuzco was dominated by ceremony and ritual, and this tradition continued in different ways through the colonial Spanish period and on to the present day. During Inca times, Cuzco's main festivals were associated with the movements of the celestial bodies, especially the Sun and the Moon, and the changing of the seasons, both of which regulated Inca social life. While most rituals dealt with agricultural matters—for example, Hatun Cuzqui (Great Cultivation), in May, celebrated the maize harvest—others dealt with the cult of the dead emperors and human sacrifice.

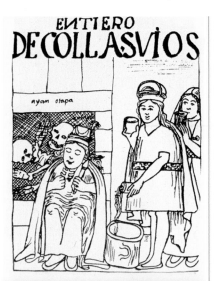

A Guaman Poma drawing showing Inca offerings at a shrine of the dead.

Capac Raymi

The most important Inca festival was Capac Raymi, or the Magnificent Festival, which took place during the first month of the Inca year, about the time of the winter solstice. Little is known about what happened at this festival, but historians do know that, as a specifically Inca event, all those not of Inca descent had to leave Cuzco during the festival. Capac Raymi included a variety of events such as the Huarachico rites of passage for young boys, the bringing into the city of the empire's tribute wealth, dancing, music, and the eating of maize cakes enriched with llama blood.

Inti Raymi

The festival of Inti Raymi, or the Feast of the Sun, was also dedicated to the worship of the Sun-god. It took place about the time of the June solstice to mark the maize harvest. The last celebration of this

The mummies of Inca rulers were paraded around the capital during the festival of Inti Raymi. They were dressed in fine clothes like the clothes on this Peruvian mummy.

Guaman Poma and other Spanish authors who wrote about the Incas tell us that the Incas made time to enjoy themselves. Athletic contests took place between sons of higher ranking Incas, and games involving dice and other games of chance were also popular. Unfortunately, no information has survived regarding the rules of these games. We also know that Inca emperors liked to hunt, and they set up game reserves. Ordinary Incas caught poaching would have faced the death penalty.

great festival took place in 1535, in the aftermath of the Spanish conquest, and it lasted about eight days. On the first day, the Inca emperor and royalty welcomed the sunrise with chanting, surrounded by temple images and the sacred mummies of past emperors. A huge feast accompanied the event, during which meat, chicha beer, and coca leaves were offered in a huge sacrificial fire. The festivities continued for a further seven days, at the end of which the emperor Manco Inca symbolically broke the Earth with a foot plow, signaling the beginning of the plowing season and illustrating the ties between agriculture and religion.

Although details of the rites of Inti Raymi are scarce in historical sources, in recent years Inti Raymi has been revived partly as an attraction for foreign tourists in search of the Inca past and partly as a day of relaxation for local Cuzqueños, or residents of Cuzco. The modern festival is sponsored and organized by local businesses, especially those involved with tourism. Local breweries have been involved. In 1980, the role of Sapa Inca was played by a hotel owner and local entrepreneur. Today's Inti Raymi has been described as 95% fantasy and 5% documentary. The dances and processions of the festival parade around Cuzco before ending up among the huge carved stones of Sacsahuaman, above the city.

This modern pottery painting shows a herd of llamas being offered to Inti, the Sun god, during the festival of Capac Raymi.

The Inca City of Cuzco

Thousands of Cuzqueños gather to celebrate the modern version of Corpus Christi.

During Inti Raymi, the Feast of the Sun, the Lord Inca, or Sapa Inca, is being carried in a litter borne by men from Rucanas. The litter is surrounded by beautiful acclas—the "chosen women"—who traditionally cared for the Inca and carried special food used in the ceremony.

Mock llama sacrifices, soccer games, picnics, and theatrical re-creations of dubious authenticity all are part of the new Inti Raymi. The invented tradition of modern Inti Raymi is recognized and acknowledged by the people of Cuzco. They see it not as an accurate re-enactment of the past but as an evocation of their city's glorious past.

Corpus Christi and Colonial Cuzco

The Spanish conquest of the Inca empire in 1532 changed the face of Inca Cuzco and led to a unique realignment of religious expression. For the Spanish, the important Christian festival of Corpus Christi was a triumphal celebration of Christ as the supreme victor over the forces of heresy, darkness, and paganism. Fresh in the minds of the Spanish was the Christian reconquest of Spain from the Moors, a Muslim people, completed in 1492. By coincidence, Corpus Christi fell between late May and early June, the same time as the Inca festival of Inti Raymi. The Spanish took advantage of this timing not only to ban Inti Raymi as a pagan festival but also to incorporate traditional Inca elements into Corpus Christi in ways that represented the Christian victory over Inca

Tales & Customs — Frozen Gifts

Archaeologists have found tiny gold and silver figures wrapped in woven cloth buried on the tops of mountains next to the frozen bodies of children who had been sacrificed to the gods. These human sacrifices would have been chosen for their great beauty and perhaps for other remarkable qualities. It was thought that sacrificing these children would bring great pleasure to the gods. This ritual did not take place often, but it was used when an emperor felt he needed extra help from the gods.

civilization and its pagan rites.

Mixed Messages

From the beginning of its celebration in Cuzco, Corpus Christi included Inca elements associated with Spanish imagery, and parts of different Inca ceremonies were reconfigured toward the worship of the Christian god. The procession of Inca "kings" was followed by images of Spanish kings, and traditional choreographed battle scenes between the Incas and their ancient enemies culminated in Inca displays of loyalty to their new Spanish masters.

The Spanish authorities allowed the Inca nobility to wear traditional Andean costumes, headdresses, and insignia during the Corpus Christi festivities. Even the wearing of Sun disks that recalled the worship of Inti was permitted because it was reinterpreted as as a sign of the triumph of Christ over Inti and of the Christian festival over the pagan Inti Raymi.

Subtle Links

Corpus Christi has been regarded as a way for the Incas to continue celebrating Inti Raymi in Christian form, but in reality, it had more subtle effects on Inca culture. It allowed the surviving Inca nobility to create a fresh role and identity for themselves in the new colonial society created by the Spanish. The success of Corpus Christi is shown by the fact that within forty years of the conquest it had become Cuzco's most important religious event.

This Christian painting from a Huaro church reflects Spanish views of Incan paganism.

CHAPTER 6

A Day in the Life of Cuzco

The unique nature of Cuzco as a city caught between several worlds—Inca, colonial Spanish, and modern—means that there are many ways to describe a typical day. For local Cuzqueños, as much as for foreign visitors, the past and the present seem to coexist at the same time and in the same place.

A Popular Place

Modern Cuzco throbs to the rhythm of thousands of tourists who flock to the city in search of a vision of the Inca past. Early in the morning, tour buses and taxis arrive outside the main hotels and whisk the visitors away on tours to nearby sites such as Sacsahuaman, the Kenko Stone, the Indian market at nearby Pisac, or the more distant ruins of Ollantaytambo. The more adventurous take a train to the ancient Inca city of Machu Picchu.

Open for Business

As the morning chill warms around the central square that was once the scene of imperial Inca festivals, dozens of tourist shops start to open for business. They sell colorful local weavings, sparkling mirrors, Inca-shaped pottery, rustic wood carvings, and engraved calabashes from the Amazon. Among the shops are bars, tourist agencies, and—a sign of the times—internet cafés.

Restaurants begin to fill at midday as locals and foreigners eat, drink, and gossip in Spanish, English, the old Inca tongue of Quechua, and a dozen other languages. Almost without noticing,

they lean against polished stones laid down five hundred years earlier by Inca masons. Visitors often try local dishes, such as the roasted guinea pig known in Quechua as cui, maize soup, or

Tourists stand on the mighty stones of Sacsahuaman.

Tales & Customs — Cuzco Weaving

The Inca people have the oldest tradition of weaving in the world. The first fabrics were produced in Peru over 5,000 years ago. Today, although most fabric in Peru is mass produced, traditional communities still make ponchos, shawls, and other clothes in the same way that their ancestors would have done. The Center for Traditional Textiles of Cuzco was set up in 1996 to ensure future generations continue to value and continue this piece of Inca heritage.

the famous chicha drink, which is also made from maize. Some tourists who find the 11,139-foot (3,395-m) altitude of the city

disorienting order coca tea, made with an infusion of the coca leaf, that calms both the head and the stomach. In the local market, Cuzqueños go about their daily business and stop to glance at the sky as another jetload of tourists are flown into the city's airport.

Late in the Day

In the afternoon, many people take an afternoon nap, or siesta. By early evening, locals and tourists again jostle on the streets

As well as knitwear, tourists can also select delicious local treats from the Cuzco market.

Street vendors in Cuzco offer tourists a variety of knitted items and a selection of jewelry.

that line the plaza mayor. In cafés and restaurants, the air vibrates with the sound of Inca panpipes and disco music and is filled with the smell of a hundred different foods. As the Moon goddess Mama Quilla rises above the square, she looks down to see her city larger, richer, and more cosmopolitan than ever. The Spanish conquest and the influence of the modern world have made Cuzco an eternal city in ways that the ancient Incas could not have foreseen.

Because the city of Cuzco is still inhabited and expanding, most archaeological excavations in its region have taken place in the surrounding and more distant areas, such as the Cusichaca Valley—situated between Ollantaytambo and Machu Picchu—and the Inca city of Machu Picchu itself. UNESCO-sponsored investigations in Cuzco since 1970 have focused on surveying, mapping, and describing surviving Inca architecture rather than excavating. Nevertheless, tantalizing glimpses of the past have emerged in recent years.

Excavations beneath parts of the Hotel Libertador have revealed traces of preimperial buildings. Below: Surviving Wari architecture at Pikillaqta, located near Cuzco.

Early Cuzco

It is certain that much archaeological evidence of Cuzco's early days was destroyed when Pachacuti rebuilt the city. People were moved out, foundations were dug, and huge new buildings were raised over the earlier settlement. When the Spanish looted the city in 1533, there is documentary evidence that, throughout the colonial period,

discoveries of Inca burials and sacred objects were still being made in the foundations of the city's major buildings and ordinary houses. Inca treasures were being uncovered in Cuzco gardens well into the 18th century. Although the archaeology of preimperial Cuzco is poorly investigated, it seems that the earliest settlements were in swampy land at the base of the hill on which Sacsahuaman was later built.

What Came Before

Archaeologists have uncovered evidence of the civilizations that settled at Cuzco before the Incas. As revealed by the huge, nearby settlement of Pikillaqta, the pre-Inca Wari civilization (A.D. 400–800), which was the first to build roads and use the quipu, was active in the Cuzco region. Archaeologists have also determined that the poorly-made Killke pottery belongs to preimperial times (A.D. 1000–1400). Several hundred sites from this period have been discovered within 37 miles (60 km) of

A Peruvian Wari mummy dressed in an unku (tunic) dating from about AD 700–1000.

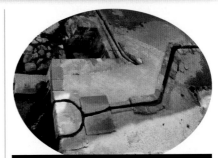

Excavations at Corichanca unearthed one of the original water fountains at the temple.

Cuzco. Killke pots have also been uncovered at various locations within the city itself, notably beneath the remains of the Coricancha temple and at Sacsahuaman. Much of what later became the imperial Inca style in architecture and pottery seems to have evolved directly out of late Killke culture, although the two styles differ in some aspects. Beneath an Inca building that is now part of the colonial-style Hotel Libertador in the city center, excavations have revealed traces of early preimperial Killke buildings that seem to be aligned according to a plan, suggesting that Pachacuti's remodeling of the city was superimposed on an existing grid.

Underground Reservoirs

During the 1930s, the Peruvian archaeologist Luís Valcárcel made preliminary excavations on the north side of the great plaza that fronts the walls of Sacsahuaman. In this area, which is dominated by the great rock called Suchuna (locally known as El Rodadero), he discovered traces of the Inca's fascination with the ritual flow of water in and around Cuzco. He found aqueducts; cisterns; underground canals, terraces, and patios; and what appeared to be an amphitheater. Between 1985 and 1986, the National Institute of Culture (INC) made more investigations in this area, and it has more fully excavated and reconstructed the "amphithe-

The Inca City of Cuzco

In the 1990s, the Peruvian government authorized the demolition of houses that stood on the site of the ancient Sacred Garden in order for an archaeological dig to be carried out.

with maize and animals made out of precious materials. The garden was built over by the Spanish, but in 1990, the Peruvian government bought this land, and in 1992, they allowed an archaeological dig to get under way. Excavations uncovered a few foundations, an Inca fountain, and some pottery. Work at the site finished in 1993, and the land was returned to its original use as a garden.

ater." It is now thought to have been a reservoir fed by local springs and an integral part of the Inca water system.

Excavations at the Sacred Garden

In 1975, work began on the reconstruction of the convent and church at the Coricancha Temple. Archaeological digs uncovered one of the five original fountains located at the temple. Water still flows through its finely carved channels. It is possible that in the future remains of the other four fountains will be found.

In Inca times, the temple stood on an artificially flattened hill between two small rivers. Where the Avenida El Sol stands today was originally the site of the Sacred Garden—a place that, according to Spanish chroniclers, was filled

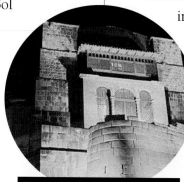

The ritual paths known as ceques all stem from the Coricancha temple.

Rediscovering Cuzco's Sacred Landscape

Between 1990 and 1995, investigations took place into the location of imperial Cuzco's sacred shrines, the ritual paths known as ceques, and their relationship to Inca ideas of the sacred landscape.

Tales & Customs — Finds in Strange Places

A valuable 18th century Cuzco painting called The Adoration of the Kings has had a strange history. After its whereabouts were unknown for several centuries, it turned up at a Cuzco's farmers market in the 1920s. While buying food at the market, a woman named Mrs. Freyer noticed some bright colors on a cushion on which a stallholder was sitting. She asked if she could have a closer look at the cushion, and it turned out to be the lost artwork, complete with patterns made of pure gold.

Archaeologists unearth an Inca skeleton at the site of Sacsahuaman, Cuzco.

Latest Discoveries

On September 29th, 2001, archaeologists unearthed the skeleton of what could have been a member of a royal Inca family that was buried within the grounds of Sacsahuaman. Archaeologists have now discovered sixteen ancient tombs dating from the Inca empire in Sacsahuaman.

Two years later, another exciting find was made down in the city of Cuzco itself. A team of investigators from Spain, using modern technologies such as radar and three-dimensional image producing software, suggested that there are tunnels connecting the former Incan temples—over which colonial churches were built—to Sacsahuaman. They have discovered the existence of huge tunnels more than 16 feet (5 m) deep under the Convent of Santo Domingo, which was built over the Coricancha. These are unlikely to have been built by the Spanish, as their catacombs were no more than 13 feet (4 meters) deep. On March 22, 2001, they accessed a crypt under an altar in the convent, which they think leads to the entrance of the main tunnel.

Both the ceques and shrines focused on the Coricancha temple of Inti—the symbolic heart of Cuzco. This recent work has shown how central Cuzco was connected to sacred places beyond the city; to the rocks, springs, and caves of the surrounding landscape; and to towers built on the horizon formed by the mountains around Cuzco's valley. Inca roads were found to pass by major shrines, linking the capital physically as well as symbolically to the furthest limits of empire. This system of real and imaginary lines also had a practical dimension in that it divided space and time in the view of the Inca elite. The responsibilities and privileges of Cuzco's royal clans, their access to land and water, and their ritual obligations to ancestors were all integrated into the ceque system. The painstaking work of archaeologists, historians, and anthropologists are beginning to rediscover these hidden aspects of Cuzco's sacred life.

Cuzco is a living museum, preserving astonishing Inca remains and colonial Spanish architecture. But it is currently under pressure caused by national and international tourism. Cuzco must deal with the need for hotels and accommodations and the building of new roads. It also needs to address problems of the drug trade, opportunities for local employment, and the managing of its Inca past. After many years of paying little attention to the sites of the city and its surroundings, city authorities and the government of Peru are now taking steps to protect Cuzco's precious heritage.

Protecting the Past

With a new financial-support plan, the national government of Peru has helped a local university begin an exciting program of purchasing and restoring Inca ruins in Cuzco. Early projects included buying a house that contained the walls of the palace of the Inca Emperor

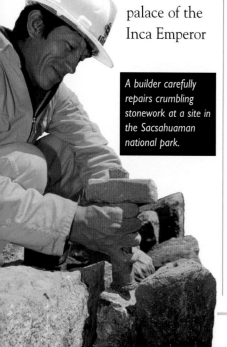

A builder carefully repairs crumbling stonework at a site in the Sacsahuaman national park.

Rocca, building an iron fence to replace the shabby mud wall that hid the famous Temple of the Sun, and making general improvements to the university's archaeological museum. Money was also set aside for Sacsahuaman, which was designated as a national park. Sacsahuaman has become the site of numerous university projects, from archaeological digs to efforts to preserve existing Incan architecture.

Arts and Crafts

As the historical and tourist capital of Peru, many weavers, pottery makers, silversmiths, and wood-carvers are attracted to live and work in Cuzco. Their works originate partly from the Inca past and partly from the city's colonial history, often skillfully

blending their twin heritage. Many artisans are based in the San Blas district of the city, and in this area are the workshops of such famous artists as Edilberto Merida and Antonio Olave. Cuzco is home to the Center for Traditional Textiles of Cuzco, which promotes traditional and innovative designs produced by a group of local villages. Using Inca and pre-Inca techniques such as the backstrap loom and local mineral and vegetable dyes, as well as more modern techniques, master textile makers use their age-old expertise to produce a dazzling array of works. As with weaving, so with pottery. Peru has a long tradition of working in ceramics, and the artisans of Cuzco and its surrounding area today produce colorful replicas of the finest Inca

Tales & Customs — International Events

The inhabitants of Cuzco involve almost everybody in their festivities. Before Inti Raymi, countless additional events take place, including street and square activities, in the daytime, and live concerts given by the very best of Peru's diverse musical talents, staged in the Plaza de Armas in the evening. Today, Inti Raymi is the second-biggest festival in Latin America, after the carnival of Rio de Janeiro, in Brazil. Most of the concerts and expositions that take place during Inti Raymi are free and sponsored by the city of Cuzco and by many Peruvian companies.

The Archaeological Museum of Cuzco is based in an old colonial house.

Inca architecture; gold, silver, copper, and turquoise idols; and objects of ritual ceremonies are all displayed for visitors to view. The collection has hundreds of Queros puyños (glass pitchers) in all shapes and sizes. There is also an important sample of colonial painting of the School of Cuzco.

Putting the Past to Work

Most of the great systems of agricultural terraces and irrigation canals that had produced bumper crops in Inca times were abandoned after the Spanish conquest. Today, however, rural populations are increasing in many areas around Cuzco, so farmers are beginning to restore and revitalize the unused land of their ancestors to provide a better future for their own children.

pottery, as well as more inventive vessels designed to appeal to international visitors. Silver jewelry—surely an echo of the imperial Inca era—rayed mirrors, and traditional musical instruments such as the quena and zampona panpipes are all locally made and sold. While such items are dismissed by some simply as tourist souvenirs, their production often draws on ancient knowledge and skills and offers a revitalized way of life for the indigenous inhabitants of the city and its area.

Many Museums

The Archaeological Museum of Cuzco is based in a colonial house built at the beginning of the 18th century and known as the House of the Admiral. Inside, the museum has many exciting Inca pieces, including stones, pottery, textiles, and the wooden cups known as keros.

Incan irrigation canals are now being put back to work by modern inhabitants of Cuzco.

aclla: a "chosen woman," also called a "Virgin of the Sun."

Aclla Huasi: the house of the "chosen women."

Amauta Inca: a teacher of young men in Cuzco, or any wise man.

Antis Inca: the name given to the tropical forest tribes; this name is the origin of the name of the quarter of the Inca empire known as Antisuyu.

Antisuyu: the Eastern quarter of the Inca empire.

Apu: an Inca lord or ruler of one of the empire's four administrative regions.

Atahualpa: the son of the eleventh Inca emperor, Huayna Capac, who fought and won a civil war with his half-brother, Huascar, shortly before the Spanish arrival.

ayllu: a lineage group or kin-based community.

cacique: the Spanish term for curaca (native chief).

camayoc: an official or craftsman.

cancha: an Inca enclosure that typically consists of rooms built around a central patio.

capac: a wealthy or influential person.

capac hucha: a human sacrificial victim.

ceque: the sacred lines of spiritual power radiating out of the Coricancha (Temple of the Sun) in Cuzco.

chasqui: an official Inca messenger.

chicha: the traditional Inca beer made from maize.

Chinchaysuyu: the northern quarter of the Inca empire.

chuño: freeze-dried potatoes

coca: a type of leaf containing a mild narcotic that is chewed by Andean peoples to allay hunger, thirst, and tiredness; also used by the Incas in religious rituals.

Collasuyu: the southern quarter of the Inca Empire.

Coya Inca: an Inca queen or high ranking woman.

Cuichu: the name given to the Inca deification of the rainbow.

cumbi: fine woolen cloth.

Cuntisuyu: the southwestern quarter of the Inca empire.

Curaca: the Amerindian principal chief of a village conquered by the Incas.

Cuzco School: the name used to refer to the Peruvian painters of various ethnic origins working in Cuzco from the 16th century to the 19th century.

El Niño: a climatic event producing torrential rains and flooding.

Huaca: a sacred place or thing; a huacas could be a mountain, freshwater spring, mummy bundle, or other place or thing.

Huascar: the official heir to Huayna Capac in Cuzco, who fought and lost a civil war against his half-brother, Atahualpa.

Huayna Capac: the eleventh Inca emperor (1493–1525).

Illapa: the Inca thunder and weather deity.

Inti: the Inca Sun god.

Machu Picchu: the Inca mountaintop city that probably served as a summer estate of the Inca emperors and was not rediscovered until 1911. Undiscovered and undamaged by the Spanish, it is the most complete example of an Inca city.

mama cunas: literally "mothers"; elder women who supervised the everyday lives and behavior of the acllas, or "Virgins of the Sun," who were young women who served as part of the Inca priesthood.

Mama Quilla: the Inca Moon Goddess.

mita: the various labor taxes that the Inca government required the Inca common people to pay.

mitmaq: people sent by the Incas to colonize newly conquered areas and aid integration into the Inca Empire.

moiety: the symbolic half or other amount into which Inca society was divided.

ñusta: an Inca emperor's daughter or a young woman of noble Inca birth.

Orejónes: literally "Big Ears"; a name used by the Spanish for high-status Incas because it describes the noble Incas' habit of wearing earlobe-plugs that enlarged their ears.

Pachacuti: literally "cataclysm," or catastrophe; the name adopted by the ninth Inca emperor, Yupanqui.

Pachamama Inca: the Inca Earth goddess.

panaqa: a royal ayllu, or clan, of male descendants.

Quechua: the Inca language.

quipu: a system of multicolored knotted strings used to record information and, possibly, historical events and songs.

Quipu Camayoc: the "Keeper of the Quipu," or an Inca administrative record keeper in charge of recording information on a quipu.

Sapa Inca: the "Great Inca"; the name for the Inca emperor.

sinchi: an Inca war chief.

suyu: a region or division, specifically, a quarter of a larger area; the Inca Empire was known as Tawantinsuyu.

tambo: a way station, storehouse, or inn located along an Inca highway.

Tawantinsuyu: the Inca name for their empire; literally, "the land of the four quarters."

Tupac Yupanqui: the son of Pachacuti who was the tenth Inca emperor (1471–1493).

Ushnu Stone: the throne used by the Inca emperor on ceremonial occasions.

Viracocha: the Inca creator deity.

yana: a servant who was often directly responsible to the Inca emperor.

Yupanqui: the ninth Inca emperor and first true Inca imperial ruler, who defeated the Chanca and established the Inca Empire (1438–1463). Yupanqui took the name Pachacuti.